THIS

Also by Dave

Man of Joy & Sorrow - all about Jesus

Mark! – a modern retelling of the gospel of Mark

John – a modern retelling of the gospel of John

No Idea

I've no idea how long this book will be – it may well be the shortest I've ever written, because I want to foolishly offer my thoughts and get outta here, mainly so that this book is a quick and easy read for you. Obviously by the time you hold it in your hands, it will be very clear how long it is. But right now, I'm just embarking on this haphazard mission, to somehow communicate the reality of Jesus, that he is full of grace and truth, that he understands our sorrows, and that he didn't come to JUDGE the world but to rescue it. I am convinced he came to help us, to affirm us and forgive us, to offer us a whole new way of life that no one ever dreamt of before. I put the word JUDGE in capitals there because that is what many of us struggle with, the fear that others are judging us.

I think I'm right in saying that when we are little many of us have an innate sense of God, and we don't perceive him as being a finger-jabbing tyrant. He's just a presence with us, perhaps expressed at times as an invisible friend.

But as we get older, and we experience the various shades of reality, and we find life is far more complex and disappointing than we first imagined, so the baggage piles up. And we no longer see God as this wondrous, creative, constant accomplice.

Feel free to scribble any thoughts or reactions or banter in these blank spaces dotted throughout this book:

Tumbleweed

It really saddens me when we get God confused with rules, regulations, and religion. Having recently watched the King's coronation it seemed apparent to me that most people in Westminster Abbey had done just that. No one much looked as if the service was a life-giving, love-affirming, creative experience. Not even when the gospel choir sang and danced their heart out. At times you might have thought the congregation was attending a watching-paint-drying event. Or a slow-motion tumbleweed contest.

I may be reading the situation incorrectly, it was after all the coronation of our new King Charles, but let's not forget, when Jesus of Nazareth rode into Jerusalem on a tiny donkey (the nearest thing to his coronation day), the place was alive, the crowd were cheering, there were no safety barriers or ear-pieced bodyguards, it was messy and surprising, and it made a whole city feel better. And as we were reminded by the Bible reading in Charlie's service – Jesus is the true King, the once and future King, the one above all others. Here's my paraphrase of that Bible reading from the book in the New Testament called Colossians.

Jesus made God visible and approachable, he was there when there was nothing, he was the beginning of all life. He was the spark of the big bang, the one who flung stars into space and set the planets spinning. He is the source of life that never runs out, even today. All the rulers, prime ministers, kings, queens, presidents, CEOs, and all of us precious, unique people, you and I, we have been wired up by him. He was around when nothing else was around, before time itself, when there was no time, no before or after. Only the present moment. He was the seed of all life in the universe. Everything we can see and everything we cannot. He put it all together. And the greatest thing is... we can get to know him. Day by day. Step by step. Little by little. The greatest king.

As I say, that reading draws on a bit of the letter to the Colossians, chapter 1 verses 15-17, and it's a pretty extraordinary reminder of which king to look to for help and guidance, strength and purpose, inspiration, affirmation, and courage.

This is the worldview offered to us by the writers of the Bible.

Image

When we give up on God it seems to me that quite often it's not about God at all, it's about the way people and circumstances have hurt us. And I think the reason we then equate people's harmful words and behaviour to the existence or not of God, is that we are all made in the image of God. This is what Genesis chapter 1 offers us. This means that when we do kind, caring, courageous things we are passing on positive messages about God, but when we do harmful, hurtful, selfish, damaging things we are passing on the idea that God is irrelevant and uncaring.

Jesus said as much. If you have a Bible and want to check this out have a look at Matthew chapter 7, in the New Testament, starting to read at verse 11. If not, here's my paraphrase of what he said. Just as you and I, flawed and self-obsessed as we are, know how to do good things, and give good gifts to others, so God knows how to do good things and give good gifts to people. In other words we have the ability to model the nature of God to the world. Smile and you show people that God smiles on them. Offer a kind word or a kind act and you show the kindness of God. Do something unselfish, creative or courageous, or all three, and so you are demonstrating that God is gracious and compassionate and stuffed full of goodness.

But when life turns on us, we can be tempted to give up on the idea of a good God. Here are three examples of that from the Bible.

Bitter

When a woman called Naomi lost everything, including her sons and her husband (her story is told in Ruth chapter 1 in the Old Testament), she arrived back in Bethlehem and told everyone she was changing her name to Mara, which means bitter. This is how she felt, and she blamed God for all that had gone wrong. 'I went away full,' she said, 'but God has brought me home empty.' What she doesn't mention here is that God has given her Ruth, a constant friend who has promised to stick with her whatever happens, even if it means death.

When Jesus was arrested, and his close friend Peter was left lost and confused, he disowned Jesus. He couldn't understand how this terrible thing could have happened, this was not what he planned or expected at all. So he gave up on Jesus and ended up crying in the dark. Nothing made sense to him anymore. You can read about this in Matthew chapter 26 starting to read at verse 69.

When the people of Israel were captured by the Babylonians and taken away from their homeland they were so disorientated they couldn't worship God anymore. 'How can we sing our songs in this strange land?' they said. Where was God in all this mess? Psalm 137 relays this cry. Their world had become detached from anything good, so they were left damaged and feeling abandoned. And their faith lay in tatters. As I said before, the writers of the Bible are crucially honest. They don't hide these moments when people lose sight of God, when they struggle to keep believing.

Three Women

1. There was a woman who had been rejected and stigmatised for twelve years. She was told she was unacceptable to people and God, and yet it wasn't her fault. She got ill in a culture where people were terrified of getting sick and saw it as a curse. So she was alienated. Pushed away, unloved, and no longer embraced. Until Jesus came to town. This woman was never unacceptable to him, never cursed by God. Imagine the scene. There are bodies everywhere, a crowd has turned out to see this new celebrity carpenter from Nazareth, this guy is trending because he tells great stories and can fix your problems. That's the word on the street anyway, so the street is packed.

And somewhere in the scrum of sweating bodies a damaged woman is nuzzling her way through. Crawling like a caterpillar, wondering if this is going to be worth it. She doesn't want to bother this celebrity carpenter, he might get annoyed. She just wants to make contact with his clothes, in the hope that some of his power might just change things for her. Her arm snakes towards him, the fingers flexed as she does her best to find the edge of his robe. That's all she wants, just a brief moment of contact. And then it happens. And she freezes. And so does he. A crackle of electricity has passed through her body. And through his too. And now for the important part. Being rejected for twelve years leaves an open wound. He's not having that. And so, in front of everyone, he calls her out. The one thing she was trying to avoid. Everyone knows she is a mess, don't call attention to it, please.

Too late. He's cleared a space and is standing there waiting. It takes a while to summon up any courage but eventually she raises a hand and shuffles forward, eyes fixed on her feet. His eyes are on her, and there is a warm smile too. 'My daughter,' he says right there in front of everyone. Declaring her clean and whole and loved by God. She raises her eyes and sees the generous welcome in his open face. He's not like all the others. He's here to welcome and embrace her. She is free. This carpenter has not come to judge people, but to rescue them. (You can read this in Mark chapter 5 verses 24-34.)

2. People talk. Of course they do. The word on the street is she is immoral. Filthy. A failure. Don't go too close you might get contaminated. She can't keep hold of her men. Perhaps she's a disappointment to them. Maybe she doesn't live right, sound right, do things right. Either way she

has been dumped by five husbands. And that was never her dream. No girl grows up dreaming of being dumped. And every time she comes to this well she's reminded of this. No one will go there with her. It's a place of pain. The water's fresh but it might as well be diseased, stagnant. And now there's another man here. A stranger lurking. She immediately tenses. What's he want? All the men she's known have been on the take. She steels herself to fetch the water as fast as she can. He's sweating, yet he offers a smile. She doesn't return it. He's saying something, asking for some water. Get your own water, she thinks, then she catches the gentle look on his face. She feels so thirsty at times, so dry inside. Ironic when she comes to get water every day. Yet life has left her empty and disappointed. She sneaks a look at him again, he's talking about some other water now, is there another source round here then? (This is a tale found in John chapter 4 verses 1-14.)

3. She comes in with her eyes lowered, her cheap make-up in smears, barely any colour left in her cheeks. She's just 'entertained' the 6th man of her day, and she's exhausted. Her young body feels like the ruptured hulk of a broken boat, beached, and left to rot. Every inch of her aches. But now, for

once, her tears don't go unnoticed, her aching loneliness is not lost. Instead her heartbreak washes the feet of this 7th man, and her tousled hair gently cleans and dries them. The room is full of spectators, appalled, intrigued, critical, leering at the bits of her life strewn before them. She could let the rage flare within her, but she has better things to do. She dares lift her eyes. She's heard stories about him, and there is a light in his eyes she's not seen before. Perhaps he is the kind of man who won't make demands on her, the first man to look at her with respect in his gaze. Her fractured heart is a war zone, but in here, drawing close to this man and willingly let her guard drop for a moment, she senses a whisper of peace. And though she is desperately cautious about it, she senses hope too. (You can read this in Luke chapter 7 verses 35-39.)

I offer these three stories because at the heart of them are three people who were judged and marginalised and ostracised in their culture. And yet Jesus cut through all of that, and treated them as precious, unique and valued people. Most of the folk Jesus met when he was on earth were poor or working class, struggling to make ends meet. He'd come from that kind of background himself and wanted to show folk that God was not for the powerful and privileged. He was for everyone. Whatever their status, background, income or ability.

The Problem

There is a problem with the world. The great gift of freedom of choice. The wonderful gift of freewill. Or rather, as we have now, freewill-gone-wrong. FGW. Or to use another initialism. RATMU. The Relentless Ability To Mess Up. We all possess that, and we indulge in it every day. (I shamelessly admit to being inspired here by Francis Spufford's initialism HPtFtU, from his great book *Unapologetic*.)

There's a flawed and self-obsessed guy in the Bible who was once known as Saul; he was hellbent on wiping out Christianity, using all means possible. Startlingly for him, he encountered Jesus on a road and lost sight of all his violent plans towards other people. And so he started again, and then he started writing letters and travelling about and meeting loads of other flawed and self-obsessed people. And instead of annihilating Christians he tried to help more and more people *become* Christians. Because it seemed to him to be the best thing ever. You can read about it in the book of Acts chapter 9, in the New Testament. And the reason I mention him is this. In one of his letters, called Romans, in chapter 7, he writes all about this great gift of freewill, and how he battles with RATMU every day. He doesn't do the things he knows he should, and instead does things he knows he shouldn't. And he ends with a cry. Yikes!! What can be done? And that's when he looks to Jesus, and he says, 'Thank God, Jesus will rescue me from myself.'

Now Saul, or Paul as he went onto be, is seen as one of the greatest communicators about Jesus. Yet he was still human, still subject to FGW, he still struggled with RATMU. Because the Bible is full of real people.

Paul also wrote, in chapter 2 verse 19 of his letter called Galatians, that he no longer felt compelled at all to try and impress us or God, he was able to look his flaws and inabilities full in the face. All because of the generous kindness and welcoming forgiveness of Jesus. 'It is no longer important that I appear righteous before you,' he is recorded as saying, in *The Message* version of the Bible, 'or that I have your good opinion, and I am no longer driven to impress God. Jesus lives in me.' That's gut-punchy stuff. He knew it was no longer about being a sorted, perfect, shiny, happy person, and could quite readily admit he was at times a loser and a bit of a mess. Join the club!

Restless

A random reading in case it's at all helpful.

Today I'm a little restless,
(there's always a bit of restlessness in my soul
but often it gets tweaked in the right direction,
towards ideas or worship or a small sea of calm.)
But today I'm a little more restless,
a little bit empty,
a little bit wondering what life is about,
a little frustrated that I don't appreciate the good
things more.
Today I find myself wandering,
trying to find home,
trying to rediscover that joy of salvation,
that first love,
that peace that passes understanding.
So today help me to sense that
You know emptiness and restlessness,
And you are with me in all of this.

Some things the Bible is not about:

The right answers

A superior attitude

A reason to view people as 'them and us'

Rules for being a perfect person

A special religious language

Some things Jesus is not about:

Floating around with a halo on his head

Pointing out people's faults

Standing with his arms open and a benign smile

Being serious all the time

Looking cool or uncool

Some things being a Christian is not about:

Getting it right all the time

Singing worship songs all day

Leaving your personality at the recycling centre

Pretending to be strong

Wearing certain clothes

Human

The thing about Jesus is he's not trying to make you and I better Christians. He's really not. Why would he? When he lived on the earth for 33 years (2000 years back) there was no such thing as a Christian. There were just human beings. So what Jesus wants to do is help us be more fully human. If, as I believe, Jesus designed humans in the first place, then he knows what makes for the best version of life in this universe. And that's what he's about. Whether or not we adopt the tag of *Christian* is up to us. Tags can be useful to help others know where to go if they sense God is starting to work in their lives. Or if we start to sense reverence humming within us, as Jane Fonda puts it on her webpage about her faith. (Sadly tags are also slapped on us in life so that other people can box us in.)

We might not understand this growing sense of reverence at first. Whoever does? Whoever could fully understand the deep call within us towards our Maker? We have brains the size of quarks compared to the solar-system-sized mind of our Creator.

But anyway, Jesus said he came to bring life, full life, and it seems to me that this by-passes religion and is way bigger than Christianity or spirituality. It's about every last single earthly blooming thing.

Apologies for the language there but some things need a *blooming* in them to press home the point.

Real life is about coffee shops, and train journeys, and loo breaks, and texting, and pubs, and helping one another through pandemics and surviving economic downturns. And everything else. And this is where the presence of Jesus can be found.

In the book of Exodus, in chapter 20, Moses was given the Ten Commandments, to pass onto a newly freed nation of ex-slaves. And the message was simple. This is how to treat life, God, and each other. In Egypt they had been herded around like property, hounded and harassed like cockroaches. So they needed to start again. To learn a new way of life. When you're a slave people can kill you and nobody bats an eyelid. They can take your possessions. Including the people you love. But life was never intended to be like that. Human beings are designed to care about people and the world. That's why we get Live-aid, and Toilet Twinning, and IJM, and Oxfam, and MAF, and Comic Relief, and Sport Relief, and the Trussell Trust, and Mother's Union, and the Big Issue, and a billion other things we may not have heard about which are making life better, rather than worse.

When Jesus was asked to sum up the best commandments in the gospel of Mark, chapter 12 verses 29-31, his reply was love God and look after each other. With all the energy you can muster.

Now if you're like me you have good days and bad days and terrible days with that. Because of the RATMU problem. But Jesus knew that. 'In this world you'll have trouble,' he said. He knew it wasn't easy. But as flawed as we are, when we do show that we care we are like signs of hope for other people. And to misquote the character of Gwen in *The Amazing Spider-Man 2* – 'Even if we keep on missing the target when we aim to show compassion, what better way is there to live?'

Which brings us back to the notion that we are made in the image of God and so are able to give each other signs of his hopeful presence in the world. Even on days when I feel smack down in the RATMU sludge and can barely rub two sticks of hope together, I'm still fairly sure that holding onto the love of God and caring about others is the best way to live.

Sophie Scholl, who gave her life in the fight against Nazism in World War Two, said this:

'I will cling to the rope God has thrown me in Jesus Christ, even when my numb hands can no longer feel it.'

Old Testament God

Recently I heard the phrase – Old Testament God – and it made me wonder. What are folk thinking when they say that? Are they thinking of Psalm 103? Or the book of Ruth? Or the line from Isaiah 41 v 13, 'Don't be afraid, I will help you… I will hold you by your hand.' You see, it's very easy to have a small idea about the Old Testament part of the Bible. It's a little like a game of Chinese whispers, as we pass on a misleading idea. 'The Old Testament is full of people killing each other and an angry God wiping everyone out with a flood. Oh and a man being swallowed by a whale which is impossible so the whole book must be made up.' That sort of thing.

The whale by the way is called a big fish and the big fish is really a red herring. The book of Jonah is actually about a prophet who secretly knows that God is kind and forgiving and therefore does not want to take that message to people he hates. He'd rather run away slash drown slash be-swallowed-by-a-red-herring slash die than take a message about a loving God to folks he despises. 'I knew that you were a gracious and compassionate God,' rants Jonah, 'slow to get angry and filled with unfailing love.' And he was clearly highly miffed. And so there you go, in the big fishy tale of Jonah it's not God who's angry with people, it's Jonah.

It's true that there is violence in the Old Testament. It fascinates me that there is a line in the book of 2 Samuel chapter 11 verse 1 about it being 'the time when kings went to war'. Indicating that just as we spring clean our houses in March, soldiers set their spears at a jaunty angle so they could head off and stick 'em through someone. But that was the way of things. It gets trickier when the writers record that God sends them into battle, but even these accounts have to be read carefully. In the book of Judges in chapter 6 God asks little Gideon to gather an army so they can throw out the Philistines. The Philistines were violent invaders, not just a bunch of folks with no taste in fashion, art, music, or interior design. However, it turns out that Gideon's army was never intended to fight and kill, but rather to scare the pants off the Philistines so that they panicked and routed and did a runner for the hills. When Gideon later went on his own rampage that was **not** ordained by God, power just went to the little man's head.

This is complex territory rooted in ancient ways and I don't want to oversimplify it here. What is clear is that God hates oppression and slavery. And the promise comes hammering home again and again that the best way forward is peace and respect. 'Let justice roll down like a river...' Amos the prophet declared in chapter 5 of his book.

Difficult

Life is difficult and I think it has always been so. And the writers of the Bible are incredibly honest, that's why the Bible is full of life's difficulties. That's why we have a book called the Psalms, which is a right old mix of people praising God, questioning God, expressing violent thoughts, pouring out their hearts, ranting on about people they don't like, and reminding themselves that God is forgiving, and gracious and patience and NOT LIKE US! And we might miss the fact that this great book of songs shows us how honest we can be with God. We can tell him how much we want to love and trust and know him, but we can also admit that we are angry and disappointed and afraid and alone.

For example, Psalm 52 reads like this year's UK Eurovision entry – a song about how someone 'done me wrong and so I'm going to sing about it'. In Psalm 52 David has a right old go at someone called Doeg who betrayed him. It's punchy stuff. And King Dave sings this song to God. As worship. Not merely so that he can hold onto that anger and keep going on about it, but so he can let it go.

There is nothing particularly 'Christian' about the advice that holding onto anger is very unhealthy. That's just good advice for life. What Jesus offers us is somewhere to take our anger and ask for the help to let it go. Not too long back I met someone who was finding it very difficult to forgive someone. Every day she prayed and every day she still felt like she hadn't forgiven them. And then one day she prayed, and she realised – she had done it, she had forgiven them. She was free, she had let it go. But it took a while.

Much of our life spent muddling along with Jesus is not about quick fixes, it's a one-step at a time thing. A marathon, not a sprint. Most of us know far less and have lots more questions and doubts than we can admit. But that's why I need Jesus, to have somewhere to take all those things. All my frustrations and embarrassments and regrets and shame and questioning and doubting and two-facedness and bad decisions and intentional wrong-doing.

Crocs

Jesus arrived on this planet… first as a vulnerable baby dependant on bumbling parents, then as a child playing with his mates in the neighbourhood, then as a teenager learning his dad's skills, then as a builder making houses and fixing furniture, then as a travelling teacher, storyteller and miracle man… to show us what God is like. To nail the colours of God firmly to the mast. God is not made of wood, or rock, or glass, or silicon, he's alive and caring and courageous and interested in us. And he knows what it is to be stuck on this wonderful and troubled planet because he has walked in our shoes/sandals/flip flops/boots/crocs/trainers etc.

God with skin on. God with nerve ends, and rings under his eyes, and favourite food, and a sense of humour, and a complexion. And emotions, and disappointments, and a personality.

A prophet in the Bible called Isaiah wrote this at the start of chapter 42 of his book: 'Look at my servant, whom I strengthen. He is my chosen one, and I am pleased with him. I have put my Spirit upon him. He will reveal justice to the nations. He will be gentle – he will not shout or raise his voice in public. He will not crush those who are weak or quench the smallest hope. He will bring full justice to all who have been wronged. He will not stop until truth and righteousness prevail throughout the earth.'

That's Jesus. Not a thing, or an idea, or a guru, or a hard taskmaster, or a philosophy. But a servant who is gentle and full of strength and courage. A person watching out for those who society judges and shuns and shoves aside. Someone who does not follow trends or peer pressure, but who understands the static in our minds and the fracture in our hearts.

To Love

To love means our heart being broken. To live on earth means an end to our earthly life one day. These are sad facts about life. I don't even want to type them here, but it's reality isn't it. And Jesus went through these things. He knew the heartbreak of rejection and misunderstanding. When things got tough his friends scarpered, one of his best friends claimed he'd never even met Jesus. When Jesus tried to help people get a fresh vision of God they kept trying to manipulate him and put their words into his mouth. The so-called experts of his age heaped criticism on him day after day. He was forever living with conflict. 'In the world you'll have trouble,' he once said, and he knew all about that. In an Old Testament book called Isaiah, in chapter 53 and verse 3, he is described as 'a man of sorrows, well acquainted with bitterest grief'. He knew pain and trouble and fear and oppression. And violence.

Though the writers tell us that he had extraordinary power, and could feed thousands of people (John's gospel chapter 6), raise the dead (John chapter 11), and lay on a massive free bar for a wedding (John chapter 2), he would not do battle with those who had come to kill him.

Power-players

Jesus challenged the power-players of his day. And though the authorities did their best to cancel him, the ordinary people loved him. So the government grew desperate and falsely convicted him of crimes against the state. And having done that they threw the responsibility for his punishment onto the invading nation that they hated – the Romans. The Romans crucified thousands of people. It was their public way of scaring the hell out of those they were dominating. And so we find that, every year, Christians get very serious about a day called Good Friday. There was nothing good about it at the time. It felt like epic-fail Friday. The man who so many people had looked to for freedom and a new start, had gone the way of all the rebels. He was pinned up on two bits of wood and left to broadcast the fact that the Romans were unbeatable. End of story.

Or was it? For those who see Jesus as a good moral teacher, this is where the roads diverge. Because he would just have died on that cross, been buried in a borrowed tomb, and to this day the followers of this good moral teacher would be making pilgrimages to see the site and perhaps take away a key ring or a paperweight as a trophy from the experience. But people don't do that. Instead they wear a cross in their ears, or round their neck, or tattooed on their arms and legs. A cross. Hmm. That shocking, stomach-churning sign of total failure... if that was merely the end.

When the writer CS Lewis (inventor of that magical wardrobe) wanted to see Jesus as a good moral teacher, his mate JRR Tolkien (inventor of that magical ring) pointed out a problem. Jesus kept alluding to himself as being the son of God. 'I am the way to God, the truth about God, and the life in God,' he said in John 14 verse 6. It was the constant subtext in all that he said and did. And then his friends started saying similar things about him too. 'Jesus is the visible image of the invisible God,' that activist formerly known as Saul wrote in the first chapter of his letter to the Colossians. So if this teacher of good moral ways was offering this description of himself, he was either telling the truth... or he wasn't. And if he wasn't then he was not a good moral teacher. He was telling porky-pies. See the dilemma? CS Lewis did.

Aslan

And that's why crosses are everywhere. Because just like Aslan in CS Lewis's book (he's the lion in *The Lion, The Witch and The Wardrobe*), death couldn't grip him. The lion was murdered on the stone table by the witch, and yet he came back to life. And Lewis based his tale on what happened to Jesus from Nazareth. There is no hallowed tomb with Jesus's bones in it. Instead there is a Good Book full of people who want to tell us what it means for Jesus to have smashed out of the grip of death. For Jesus to be alive now.

So the cross of Jesus is not like all the other thousands of crosses the Romans used. It represents a new way. A different life. Eternal life. A promised future of peace and harmony going on forever. Wearing a cross is barbaric when you think about it. Like wearing a hangman's noose around our neck. Or having a tattoo of an electric chair. Except that the cross became a symbol of life not death. It became the place where you and I can go and let go of the stuff that is weighing us down, hurting us. The stuff that other people pile onto us. The hurt and judgement. A place we can visit every day.

I carry a little wooden cross in my pocket. It's been carved by a friend of mine and it's not perfect. But that's the point. It's not about the cross itself, it's about what it means, what it represents. Roman crosses were coarse, gnarly, bodily-fluid-stained things. But a cross is just a cross like any other cross… until one man hangs on it. And then it can mean the world to us. I have dozens of names printed in a tiny font on a bit of paper and sellotaped around my pocket-cross. And every day I can bring those people to Jesus as a prayer, simply by taking hold once more of the cross that I need so much.

Small

When we look up at the night sky
And see the breath-taking work of your hands,
We wonder - what are people that you should care for us?
When we feel small and inadequate,
Powerless and easily swayed.
When we wish we could be heroes,
Yet find ourselves adrift in a sea of straying,
We wonder once again,
What are people that you should care for us?
When we find ourselves in a land of giants,
When others seem to ignore us,
Or disregard us, or let us down,
When we fail to make the kind of impact we long for,
We wonder once again,
What are people that you should care for us?
When we hear again that ancient story,
Truth and love pinned on a darkened skyline,
A kind courageous man held before us with three nails,
And we wonder why he would go so far for us,
We ask once again,
What are people that you should care for us?
We wonder again about that love,
The love so far beyond our understanding,
Bigger than our frequent mistakes and our little minds,
Small enough to reach into every crevice of our lives,
And we wonder once again,
What are we that you should care for us?

Magic Eye

I think that faith in Jesus can be a bit like looking at one of those *Magic Eye* or *Stereogram* pictures. Remember those? You stare at them for a while and you can't make sense of them, but if you look for long enough, and give it some time, slowly the image emerges, and things become clearer. You can find a few of these on the old world-wide-interweb.

It's a little like that with the Bible and Jesus, things may not make much sense at first, but with a little time and a prayer for some help, you may find that the words about Jesus start to come off the page and seep into your mind and life a bit.

I remember having my first Bible and flicking the pages with a sense of being locked out, but when God began to work in my life the book came alive to me. Oh, and if you're not into reading there are Bible Apps out there – *YouVersion* is one – so you can listen to various Bible bits. You don't have to be a reader. You can also watch episodes of the series *The Chosen* on the *YouVersion* App, so you can watch stuff about the life of Jesus too.

The House on the Edge

(A kind of parable)

She lived on the edge of town, almost so far out that folk never quite knew where they were when they stumbled into her cottage. When I say stumbled it wasn't as if people weren't looking for her, they were, but in finding her the house appeared to be in a different location every time. They came with their grievances, their angst, their crises, and distress. Their longings, wishes and dreams. And they told her all about these, because, after all, she was so far removed from their daily lives that there was no danger of her passing their cries onto others and thereby embarrassing them.

Some folks poured out their souls and then wandered away again, some of them even breaking off in mid-sentence. Others brought the same pleas day after day. Some came once a year, others once a week, some ten times a day. Some hurtled in and out as if their houses were on fire. Some came to shake their fists. In anger, frustration, sadness or all three. And some discovered that, as they talked and cried and muttered and sang, somehow their perspective changed, and it was as if they had found a solution, or perhaps not a solution, but another step, another thought to lead them on.

Some found answers of course. But many found something else. Comfort, strength, direction, a smile in their pain. And some found that the silence was in itself a kind of healing balm. So many people, so many visits, in so many different ways. And she said relatively little, perhaps nothing at all, and yet she said so much. A different kind of language. Some claimed she was not there at all, others that she had been there once, but had now moved away. But even some of those people found themselves stumbling across her doorstep, their questions and convictions in their hands, like a flurry of toys and discarded clothes gathered up from the carpet of a messy house.

She lived on the edge of town, almost so far out that folk never quite knew where they were when they stumbled across her. And she loved everyone who came. Though the cost to her was great at times. The burdens of these people were frequently heavy. So, she was grateful for those, often children, who came with their laughter and jokes and smiles and discoveries. Offering these silly and sublime treasures in their bright and jumbled conversations.

I don't have it all figured out

I love life but it scares me
I believe in hope but sometimes despair
I believe in caring but sometimes folk bug me
Some days I like them some days I don't
Sometimes I think I'm winning
Sometimes I feel as if I'm losing
Because I don't have it all figured out yet
I want to smile but often scowl
I long to be upbeat but find myself complaining
Want to be understanding but frequently judge
I want to help but often hinder
Some days I seem to have all the answers
Some days I don't have any at all
Because I don't have it all figured out yet
I know what I think and then I don't
I have my principles then lose them
I want to fight for truth and justice
Then I want to throw in the towel
I know where I'm heading then
Feel suddenly lost all over again ...
Because I don't have it all figured out yet

Don't Give Up

None of these words will amount to much really unless God takes them and uses them to help whoever is reading them. So that's my prayer. My words represent a cumbersome, clunky, awkward attempt to describe something that I believe is the most precious thing in the universe. Something that is not about rules, religion, or regulations. Something which is about every single part of life.

'See how much our God loves us,' a guy called John wrote, in chapter 3 of his first letter in the New Testament, 'he loves us so much he has made us his children.'

What's that mean? For me? For you? For them? Different things to be honest. I pray that little by little you and I can discover the wonder and the reality of its meaning, day by day, night by night, challenge by challenge, smile by smile.

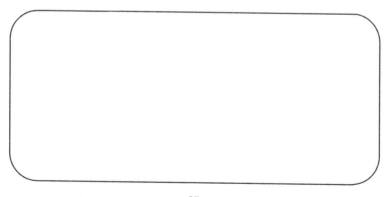

A Prayer If it's Useful

Lord, I don't have the answers, I know what I think about some things, but I am confused about others. I don't see clearly who you are and what that means for me, and I have no idea where following you will lead. But please help me to take a small step with you today. Open my eyes a little more and heal my heart and mind so I can trust you enough for the next chapter of my life. Amen.

Blue Sky Thinking

'I look up at the sky and see the vast work of your hands, and I know you care for us...' Psalm 8

We open our eyes, to remember, to look up, to see again... this vast and floating world we inhabit. Stopping. Looking. The colours, the shades, and hues. The sun chasing the clouds, the clouds fighting back. The moon shooing the day away, the dawn seeping wonder across the fading gloom of night. The quiet shuffling of those ragged white cloudy pillows. Unhurried. Dallying. Gliding with their awesome gentleness. Reminding us we are small yet intensely significant.

Wonder

'When I notice once again, the sparkling glimpses of life in another day's trudgery...'

Those small moments, when we catch our breath, smile, laugh unexpectedly. Those glimpses of the precious nature of life. Those views, those reminders of the size of everything. Of the vast nature of the universe. And the treasured nature of people. Those things that take us back to the days of childhood, when the world was new to us, when we explored and discovered and freely and regularly gasped.

Don't
Give
Up

Don't
Give Up

41

Printed in Great Britain
by Amazon

44743642R00030

The Ice Castle of Bavaria

By

Farhan Bhatti

Intro:

Welcome to my wacky world, within this book you will find the first part for this story. I would like to thank all those who believed in me and helped encourage me to finish this book without you this book would never have been published. For your own enjoyment please sit back relax, put the kettle on and enjoy reading the stories written until the next book comes out.

With front cover design from Canva

"Just because you pass or accomplish something in one try does not mean you are perfect there's still room for improvement."

Contents

Chapter 1: The journey

The ice castle located in Bavaria Germany, home to many people in the small town of Schwangau. Legend has it, that many people who have stayed in the ice castle have never been seen again; or have never been able to live to tell the tail until now. Said Cupcake talking to Krazy while packing her bags ready to move in with Krazy and the gang into the Ice castle of Bavaria. They travelled across the Atlantic Ocean by boat for 2 months to then hire a car which would take them to the ice castle where they would meet up with the rest of the gang.

The ice castle from the outside was surrounded by snow and trees deep in the woods, once they had reached the ice castle, they settled in waiting for Bella, Ron aka Jeff and Kinky to arrive at the castle. They could hear strange noises coming from the castle, deciding to split up and search for the mysterious sounds, the castle was covered in paintings probably worth millions or more with spider webs and dust upon dust as if no one had ever cleaned them or even removed the painting from when they were originally placed around the castle.

While the two of them were wondering around Darth was in his chambers with his two companions, Scotch was one of them who was also his right hand man, it was only a matter of time until they too could hear some noises but this time coming from outside. Bella, Jeff and Kinky now arrived at the castle only to find no one was home?

They thought the castle was completely abandoned or possibly they arrived at the wrong destination, it was already too late for them to recall their cab as it had already left, but a strange butler was waiting at the front of the stair's. Meanwhile Cupcake and Krazy came across Jasper in the frozen exotic garden who surprisingly had an axe in his hand and face covered in what seemed to be blood…… Krazy and Cupcake gazed at each other in fear possibly knowing Jasper could be the reason behind the weird sounds.

"It's not what it looks like" replied Jasper.

As he got closer to the two of them, Cupcake ran in fear knocking Krazy to the ground for Jasper. Meanwhile back in the castle Kinky, Bella and Jeff come across the mysterious man, he looked shady with tea bags around his eyes which looked as if he would sleep for days possibly months or even years.

"Who are you?". Asked Jeff with drips of urine coming down his pants as he spoiled himself.

"I'm Coffee, one of the butlers of this castle, I'll show you three to your rooms" he replied.

The trio followed him around the castle for a tour of the castle and shown where they will be staying the gents were separated from the ladies, meaning Jeff would get scared at night as Mr Teddy was away. Before it became night Darth, Minx and Scotch left their rooms creeping around the castle looking for anything they could possibly sell or take back home with them as a souvenir, they bumped into Cupcake who looked disturbed.

"What is the matter, why are you running? Asked Darth trying to calm Cupcake down.

"It was Jasper, he had an axe, has probably killed Krazy and is on his way now as we speak". She replied with fear in her eyes.

Jasper was coming up the stairs.

"Cupcake come out and play!!!". He shouted repeatedly.

They hurried back to their chambers before Jasper could find and kill them, Minx met with Bella to obtain some poison to Kill Scotch who she did not get along with, what she did not know was which drink she had put it in to serve them both some green tea. Meanwhile Kinky had run into Jeff (Ron) while searching for the others, they could hear footsteps coming towards them very squeaky footsteps…It was only Coffee the butler.

"Dinner will be ready shortly if you'd like to follow me to the main dining room" he said.

As they followed him slowly behind. Bella, Minx, Darth, Jeff, Kinky and the others entered the large dining room, covered in decorations only available in the ice region which made the room sparkle as if they were in a disco ball. Different paintings and other decorations could be seen hanging on the walls and ceiling with the feeling of the painting's eyes following everything you did even if it were to move your head or walk around the room.

Mary the maid brought the main courses and starters to the table.

"For our main course we will be having roast chicken specially cooked by the best chief in our land" said Coffee.

Chapter 2: Unexpected cuisine

He pulled the cover off to reveal to the guests in the room something which was not chicken on the plate but a head of one of the other maids Maryse, Cupcake entered the room only to see Jasper and a few other ghostly figures hanging from the chandler. As the ghostly figures dropped from the chandler it then came clear they were not moving......but dead. Jeff went closer to inspect the bodies they rose up and started to move they all ran in fear, but Darth needed his chicken so quickly went back and took the chicken in the right container stuffing it into his pockets slowly moving backwards to run away. They ran from one room to another, top to bottom until they came across a room which they never encountered before.

Darth ate the chicken as if it were KFC Friday licking his fingers and even the plate giving Scotch the leftover bones, once they had caught up with their breath from running and Darth had finished his chicken, Bella had gone missing.

Had she got lost while running or captured by Jasper???

"Where has Bella gone" said Darth.

Pulling out some more food he stuffed into his pockets from earlier. They all looked at each other puzzled not knowing what to do next, behind Minx was a weird flashing light coming from a mysterious door, Kinky pushed Jeff to move forward, Minx managed to jump out of the way before Jeff went flying through the door down the long narrow stairs.

THUMP!! THUMP!! THUMP!! Smack!!

"Are you alright Jeff" said Kinky.

The rest poking their heads around to see where he had landed, luckily he landed on a couch but had ripped his pants to reveal his anime pants from SAO (Sword Art Online). The room had many doors with different names and sizes with a couch and a table with one candle in the middle of the room, spider webs could be seen everywhere freaking out Minx and Kinky. Darth laughed in humour as he found it amusing until he saw he had run out of chicken.

"Which door do we go through" said Cupcake everyone jumped up in fear almost causing Jeff to almost wet himself.

"Where did you come from Cupcake?" said Darth popping his head over Jeff.

"I was with you guys remember" replied cupcake

"That's right she was" replied Scotch almost half to death now.

"We should probably split up into different rooms once we find which are the exits, we can escape this place" said Cupcake.

They did as she said and split up into three groups: Kinky & Jeff in the first room, Cupcake & Darth in the second room, Scotch & Minx in the last room. As the three groups went into the rooms they were told to investigate, the candle enlightening the room had gone out, a very loud scream could be heard and once the light came back on Scotch was beaten with Krazy in the room. The whole room went silent as Krazy was in the room blocking the only exit unless they went through one of the three other mysterious doors.

Krazy twisted his neck walking towards Kinky making his arm expand to grab her, but he fell flat on his face stone cold with an axe on his back. The group were about to ask questions of how he found them until they could hear footsteps rushing down the stairs it was Jasper and his crew. They decided to split up again this time, Bella & Scotch, Kinky & Jeff & cupcake, Minx & Darth.

The room Kinky, Cupcake and Jeff entered was quite strange as it contained items Kinky recognised from her own collection at home, with different toys and objects scattered everywhere almost like a kinky room and very strangely Mary tied up. With a gust of force, the door closed behind Cupcake, Jeff and Kinky also trapped inside knew either this could be ghosts or possibly the end. They freed Mary from the table she was tied on and waited for the others perhaps someone from outside the room could open the door. Mary went to the door to keep an ear out encase someone would discover them and to act as a decoy.

Minx now appeared waiting for the moment to strike Scotch down for good, but behind her was a shadow which belong to only one man they were trying to escape from... Jasper. Minx turned her head glimpsing at the shadow and who it belong to, running for her life pushing Jeff from the side door which goes into the other room out of the kinky doorway into the same room of Scotch & Mary, Minx and Jeff were now all trapped in the same room with Jasper.

They all looked at each other not knowing what to do, where to move or how to escape, Jasper moved around in circles trying to round up everyone in the corner like baby cattle ready to be slaughtered for the market. The door was still opened if only one of them could distract Jasper while the rest could break free, thought Scotch trying his best to get his trousers back on after having an accident. Jasper threw his arm out trying to cut or at least graze someone with his knife managing to dissect Jeff's penis into two, Minx took this as an advantage to strike Jasper down, but Jasper knocked her off her two feet crashing into the hard wall.

Jasper rushed towards Minx with his knife at point end ready to kill.

BANG!!!

Jeff with whatever energy he had left in him smacked Jasper on the head with a head butt to the back knocking them both out, Darth and Bella entered the room to find Jasper and Jeff on the floor with a pile of blood surrounding them, the first thing which came to their heads was someone trying to kill them and what happened to Minx and the rest.

Darth and Bella eyes looked around the room to try and figure out what exactly had been going on, Minx woke up from her knock out from Jasper and helped Jeff to sew his little Jeff back on. It took a few attempts to put it in the right place, but she knew what she was doing with the rest giving her a hand, Scotch and Darth used the rope from the other room to hold Jasper down, putting him away in the kinky room locked from outside is what they thought.

They moved on from the kinky room to a door which led to the cold wildness of outside, what shocked them was it was not even cold or covered in snow but sunny surrounded by the sea. Jeff rubbed his eyes trying to figure out if what he was seeing was real or just his daily fantasies from a dream. A strange man with two heads, bodies and legs was approaching them. It was a Greymore and Ragna mixed in one, as they got closer they could see that they had spikes in their hands.

Chapter 3: Mystery world behind the door

Out of nowhere, more Greymore and Ragna hybrids were approaching them only this time coming full speed at the group throwing their spikes, the door behind them had shut, they were trapped. They tried pushing, barging, humping (yes Jeff thought humping the door would work) crawling but nothing seem to be working. It was no use no matter what they did nothing seemed to be working, unless someone was to open the door from the inside. From the other side of the door someone was walking towards it, the doorknob began to flourish and turn hope was restored but who came out of the door did not make the situation better, it was Jasper Free and untied. The spikes from above were starting to get closer in range.

Spikes from every angle were being thrown at them like hail stones, they all decided to run for it dodging as many spikes as they could sadly Scotch had taken a few to the knee, Minx tried her hardest with Mary's help to heal Scotch, but it was futile no good with the medical kit she had with her as it wouldn't stop the bleeding, Scotch face had started to go pale almost the same colour as little Jeff being stuck back on to Jeff. One of the Ragmores found the group hiding behind the boulder, luckily Kinky knocked it out cold for Darth and Bella to dispose of it, Jasper was starting to work with the Ragmores earning their trust to search and kill the group, they all knew it would only be a matter of time until they found them.

Tip toeing one by one carrying the injured into the deep forest, which was the only way they could travel, until they could think of a plan to sneak back to the door which transported them here to lock Jasper away for good. The forest contained many bugs, creatures, and plants you wouldn't expect to find in any museum, garden centre or science lesson, with the creatures and plants able to change their appearance and mimic anything they see hear to sound like their prey to make hunting very easy. A few times trying to trick the group into taking the bait, Jeff was caught a few times by the plants as they would change their appearance into his favourite teddy bear or pretend to be a lost girl that needed his help, but he would always be freed from the traps or saved before they could devour him by Darth.

As day turned into night the gang knew it was time to somehow sneak back to the door, Cupcake creped carefully around to make sure the close was clear and not to be noticed by either Jasper or the Ragmores to report back to the rest it if was safe to make their move. Jeff and Darth helped Scotch to move while the rest followed with rocks and a few spikes whatever they could find lounging around to fight back if they saw any enemies. Some of the Ragmores and Jasper were coming their way, they quickly hid in the bushes, Jasper smelt the air, poking the bush they were hiding in, Jeff was about to make a sound as it was poking him up the rear end but Kinky and Minx covered his mouth just in time before he could leap out screaming.

"They're over there, I can hear something" said one of the Ragmores.

The gang thought they had been spotted but instead it was a false alarm, once they disappeared they got back on their feet and started to move again, two Ragmores were guarding the door and had spotted them, before they could sound the alarm Minx and Mary had took them out, Bella helped them to dispose of the bodies once again, Darth was about to open the door.

"Can't I open the door?" asked Cupcake smiling.

"I guess, why not" replied Darth.

Stepping back to allow Cupcake to open the door. Its open they were all happy and glad they could finally escape Jasper and the Ragmores.

"Hurry Cupcake come inside before they spot us" said Kinky.

Cupcake never moved.

"Cupcake what are you doing we need to hurry"!! said Darth.

"They are over here!!!" Cupcake shouted from the top of her gingerbread lungs, Ragmores and Jasper all jumped out from the shadows from under the moon, Cupcake had betrayed them.

As soon as Cupcake had given away where they were, Jasper and the Ragmores came out of hiding from the shadows they surrounded them in a circle with their spears at point end ready to assault anyone who now tried to speak or escape. They tied them up and carried them on long bamboo logs until they could get back to the Ragmores cave filled with other prisoners, the cave had prison cells everywhere from the ground to the very top, heavily guarded making it almost impossible to escape unless you knew someone from the outside. The cave even contained cave paintings and statues of a man, on closer inspection they could see the paintings and statues were of Coffee, perhaps he was the one who found them and gave them a new home.

They separated the men from the women throwing them into different cells chaining them together, anyone in the past who had attempted to escape was left to die until they were just bones so their body could be used to warn other escapees or to feed their wild starving pets.

"You can't do this you be hearing from my lawyer!!!" shouted Scotch and Mary.

Darth tried to break the cell with his bare hands even throwing in a few headbutts, but it was futile. Jeff sat in the corner of the little bathroom they had in the cell with his socks covering his hands to make hand puppets that would growl weird noises almost sounding like Minx stomach growling for hunger. Meanwhile in the other prison cell, Kinky, Bella and Minx sat in their cell trying to come up with a plan to break out. Cupcake was coming down the hall, once she went passed their cell, they grabbed her by the hair trying to kill her for turning against them. Five of the Ragmores came rushing down and helped push and beat them down to separate them.

"I had to do it. It was the only way" said Cupcake.

She marched away into the pitch-black fog with the other Ragmores, luckily Minx managed to get one of the keys from Cupcake. Once the lights were out in the cave prison the ladies lit a torch which Kinky sneakily managed to hide they tried to break the cage door, but it would not work, they could hear footsteps coming down the hall, quickly running to put the fire out with toilet water they had in their cell. The person at their cell was no other than Cupcake with a shiny small object in her hand.

As cupcake drew out the shiny small object, Mary mouth opened wide as she was about to release the loudest scream which could wake up everyone in the cell, Kinky covered her mouth just in time and calmed her down. The small mysterious object Cupcake had in her hands was the key to their freedom. She unlocked their cell, they gazed back in confusion, why was she helping them escape?

"I had to trick Jasper into making him think I was on the same page as him so we all could escape and get the other guys out of here as well" said Cupcake handing over the gent's key to Minx.

Minx rushed as quickly as she could to the gent's cell to let them free and to be reunited with Darth, once she did they all escaped the Ragmores prison cave slowly closing the door which bought them to this chaotic place. Hopefully to finally end their troubles and fears with Jasper and his gang. As they were approaching closer to the door Jeff accidentally set off a trap set by them which signalled to the Ragmores and Jasper.

THE PRISONERS HAVE ESCAPED!!!!!

They ran for their lives as if there was no tomorrow, forcing one leg in front of the other. The Ragmores started throwing and firing their spears once more, they were almost at the door all they had to do is open that door and shut it behind them once they had entered, Scotch was slowing down the spears from a while ago were causing some heavy damage on him.

Minx and Bella turned around to see what happened, why had he slowed down? He took a spear to the knee, Mary and Darth were going to run back for him, but the spears were gathering in numbers very quickly making spear clouds that could block out the sun. They only had two options leave him behind or no matter what happens to them go after him. They knew what they had to do, Minx knew herself what choice she would have pick as well especially if it was Scotch.

Despite Minx resentment towards Scotch, she recalled Darth and Mary, going after him herself pushing and slaughtering the Ragmores out of the way trying to save Scotch in time for them to return back to the castle through the door. A few cuts and bruises but Minx just made it in time before Scotch could get his head chopped off by Jasper. Jeff, Kinky and Mary went through the door managing to break off the chains locking the door whereas Bella and cupcake held the door open defending it off from the Ragmores as Darth had ran off to help bring Scotch back in one piece.

Jasper and two other Ragmore hybrids battled Minx defending Scotch and herself long enough until Darth could come and aid them, he managed to wound the two Ragmores to retreat back into the shadows, but Jasper wanted more blood and power. Jasper fought both Minx and Darth at the same time trying to weaken them for his last strikes, slicing Darth's arms and legs for him to fall onto the ground bleeding heavily, Minx tried to help him, but Jasper kept pulling her away to fight, she fought with all the strength she had left until Jasper finally cut her down grabbing her by the throat to strangle her. Darth watched from the ground unable to stand but crawl on the ground, Jasper violently charged kicks at Darth's back and chest causing the air in him to come out, stretching out one leg to stand on top trying to crush his ribs chocking Minx with his hand.

Meanwhile as Bella and Cupcake rotated back and forth defending the door from the Ragmores they could see from the distance Minx and Darth were struggling to rescue Scotch from Jasper, they had to do something to help their companions.

"Go, help them we can do our part and fight as well" said Kinky, Jeff and Mary.

Bella handed the three of them spears scattered around them from the creatures they perished and went to help her friends.

Chapter 4: The Battle of looks vs strength

Minx tried to break free of Jaspers tight grip, but it was futile causing her to struggle even more, she was almost about to pass out. Scotch took one of the spears stuck in his leg out although it was painful half of the spear came out and was sharp like a spike, he had to stop Jasper no matter what it took. While Jasper's back was turned Scotch with the little energy he had left got up and galloped towards Jasper stabbing him in the back releasing Minx from his tight grip and falling onto the floor allowing Darth to breath once again.

Blood was scattered everywhere on the ground along with different bodies, Darth's body was too heavy to move and all three of them were badly hurt. Bella finally came rushing in the wounds Scotch and Darth had were deep and not going to be easy to fix as they did not have the right equipment on them but for now all they could do is at least help and give them clean water to wash the wounds before they could be infected.

The four of them walked slowly across the battlefield beach pushing back any Greymore remaining out of their way followed by a silent blow of the wind to block out their screaming once their daggers had gone through their delicate bodies, they came from each direction and crawled on the ground to kill the group but ended up losing their own lives against them. Minx, Bella, Scotch and Darth were now almost there they could see it in the horizon with the touch of fate being restored in them, they could smell and feel the cold now approaching from the ice castle.

The Ragmores were finally retreating as they were losing in numerous numbers, Cupcake greeted them with love and kindness along with the other three who were defending the door until they could come back, but they could hear something coming from behind and with a group of Ragmores on a large green creature an 8000 foot Genotorius with four scale bony legs, two heads and arms almost as long as an mountain with Jasper on its shoulder shouting out commands for it and a few Ragmore hybrids to follow.

They galloped for their lives trying to outpace the Genotorius but with the weight from having to carry Scotch and Darth it was no use as the large creature would soon catch up to annihilate them in one strike, Jeff and Kinky rushed towards the ginormous monster attempting to distract the Genotorius attention from chasing after Darth, Minx, Scotch and Bella. It successfully worked as it changed cords but threw Jeff and Kinky in the air through the wide-open small door with Kinky landing right on top of Jeff's back leaving an imprint.

The monster was metres away allowing the group to now make their move, they were almost at the door, Cupcake rushed towards the gang and helped them to carry Darth across the field, out of nowhere as they was walking towards the door the Genotorius came out and spotted them chasing them down narrowing the distance between it and the small gang, they had to hurry, they needed a miracle.

Closer and closer it got only a few yards away now from the door its hand expanded to the size of the London eye, they made it through the door all in one piece.

Cupcake!!!! Shouted Mary

Cupcake had been caught by the creature, pulling her back with the door closing behind them very slowly, they gazed at the remaining view they had beyond the door, the creatures other hand appeared and slaughtered Cupcake with the last image being her crumbled body being thrown into its mouth.

They looked on in shock and disappointment how could something so terrible as this happen to them when they were just inches away from being safe and sound from the terrors of Jasper. Kinky and Bella helped Jeff and wrapped him up in bandages almost making him look like an ancient Egyptian mummy while Minx and Mary helped Darth and Scotch to get back in shape so they could carry on their journey, but both needed to get some recovery as soon as possible to not risk aggravating their wounds.

They went back to the Kinky room and brought out a few pillows and covers for the group to sleep in overnight with a small campfire as the door above was locked what they did not know about the material they were going to be sleeping in was that it is haunted Xena clothing known in the ice kingdom as clothing which could turn you mad, crazy or cause no affect. As they slept near the cosy campfire Bella was seeing weird visions, the visions in her dream were a repeat of what had happened her coming through the door last just before Cupcake could come through herself repeating the words

"Murderer" "selfish" "the worst friend".

To Bella it almost felt as if it were actually happing in front of her and not in a dream, she could see the tragic event being repeated again and again, with the smell and taste of fear rushing in her skin, the screaming of Cupcake as she was grabbed from underneath her skin and the weird feeling as if it was all her fault.

Minx as well was seeing visions of Cupcakes late death from the Genotorius, almost making her turn crazy with fear and anxiety while sleeping, her heart pace was moving slowly and she was starting to get hot, she woke up in shock and sweat realising it was all just a dream. Darth had a similar dream, but it was about him almost losing his life to Jasper and Minx swooping in to save him, his breathing was stable but to him the event felt as if it was repeating itself, waking up a few minutes later after Minx.

The next morning, they all woke up with the haunted Xena clothing nowhere in sight only leaving a trace of sand and a burning smell, they all made their way back up the stairs noticing a message stuck by a machete on the door.

"One of you can die for one to return".

They all looked at each other and all rushed back to the door which saved them it was crumbling into millions of tiny little pieces with one person standing there with a large blood red axe it was Coffee.

"You can save your friend but one of you will have to give up yours" he said.

They looked around the room, who would volunteer to do it? Who would be brave enough to do it? No one replied and tried to look for another way to save her.

"I guess we are going to have to do it the old fashion way" he said reaching into his pocket throwing a small round ball into the air which illuminated the room with a spark.

"All of you will take part in a mini game I like to call Constantine; in this game all of you will take part making the chances for all of you even facing your own fears" said Coffee.

Once Coffee clicked his fingers they all fell asleep into chairs which came out of the ground, in their own fears it was set up in an arena with a small room identical as if it were actually happening in the castle, Jeff was first to take on his fear of being an women in his hello kitty pyjamas being chased by hairy muscular men, Kinky also defeated her fear of someone else in the group dying and could see Darth in the distance.

Minx fear was of not saving Darth in time from any danger she managed to overcome her fear and saw Darth was struggling, she ran towards him, Darth had the fear of Jasper almost killing him; the Jasper in his dream was much stronger and had demonic features with fire coming from his eyes. Coffee had stopped them from helping him and made them wake up while Darth, Scotch and Mary were still in his, they could see the sweat pouring down his face and his face cringing. The demonic Jasper face was changing to a more normal familiar face now in Darths dream and that person was of Bella with a knife in her hand and standing over Darth getting closer and closer.

She had gone mad and loss all human emotion which she had left, they had to stop her before she killed Darth, running as quickly as they could to help him and managed to separate them both. They all woke up back in the kinky room sat up in their beds, Bella had the knife from the dream in her hands with the dagger pointing in the direction of her chest, stabbing it right through her dark poisoned heart, Coffee laughed and disappeared in the dark foggy mist he had lied about one of them coming back to life and instead made the group become smaller. After putting the pieces together that's when they realised Coffee was the person behind everything that was happening at the ice castle.

With 6 people of the group now left and victims lives being taken the group needed to change their plans of bringing back those who have died back from the dead, to instead escape this chaotic ice castle for good. They gathered their belongings together and packed their bags for war against Coffee and whatever his next trick may be, marching in a single file to the front door, but Coffee was there, they ran to the back and all the other possible doors to escape but he was there too it was almost like he could teleport from one place to another.

"None of you will escape the castle until one remains" Coffee said making their bags disappear.

As they all moved from the back room to the front, in synced they moved one leg forward, the hard marble ground beneath their feet started to shake violently and crumble one by one eventually making the small, crowded area the group were in fall apart as well falling through the air, falling faster and faster through the air they could see laying on the ground were cages, shackles and traps all laid out.

Before they could hit the ground they looked around, grabbing on to anything in plain sight they could lock down on for safety, Mary's fingers on the metal cage had slipped causing her to fall flat onto the floor, the others watched from the cages they were on top of. Coffee was pulling them down with a magical force as if he had an invisible giant human magnet forcing them into the cages. Holding tightly with the fear of fighting for their dear life to survive, Coffee lifted Mary from the ground and tied her up in shackles in the centre of the floor for the others to see.

From the shadows Coffee brought out a large metal box and lowered the other five cages for a closer look at what he was about to do next, from the box he pulled out a large knife and stabbed it right through

Mary's shoulder twisting it as the knife went deeper into her body for the pain and agony to build up.

"Stop, pick me instead leave her, she's done nothing wrong" said Scotch.

Coffee pulled the knife out of Mary and rushed towards Scotch pushing him against the cage and making the size get smaller.

"Make it tighter you donkey this is nothing compared to everything else I've been put through" said Scotch as Coffee increased the pain.

"For that I'll make another suffer" said Coffee.

He ran towards Minx, but Darth swung his cage in front of her allowing Coffee to poke him in the arm it dug in very deep, as Coffee walked away back to torture Mary, Darth started making his cage swing backwards and forwards making Jeff feel seasick for it to finally break down the middle so he could pull out the knife put through his arm into Coffee's leg.

Coffee went down in agony onto the concreate floor, Darth took this as an advantage to steal the key from around Coffee's neck to free the others, once freed they had to find their way out and found a few others locked up in the prison cells in the ground: Jess, Duke, Crow and Cinder. They freed them and tried looking for a way to escape, noticing a light peeping throw the door to a hidden room much like the room they had once visited before in the ice castle which took them to the hot island.

This time it was different once they had gone through the door it took them outside.

Outside at last.

They were free Darth, Minx, Scotch, kinky, Jeff, Mary, Jess, Duke, Crow and Cinder all walked out breathing in the fresh air brushing off the door on to their faces. They ran through the snow-covered trees and bushes as the snow above was still falling, remembering the good memories they had before coming to the castle and the friends they had in the beginning.

Running from one side to another, until they all finally regrouped in the middle ready to say their goodbyes to one another by hugging, Jess and Cinder hugging Kinky, Duke and crow hugging Minx, but when Jess and Cinder hugged Mary while Duke and Crow hugged Scotch their faces had oddly changed they reached into their pockets digging for something. Once they clutched onto what they were searching for they took it out at light speed unknown to the human eye pushing the others back and stabbed Scotch and Mary the blood oozing life through the hole in their stomachs by the knife which tore them apart.

Duke, Jess, Cinder and Crow rushed off into the woods chased by the others as they had stabbed Mary and Scotch following the footsteps they left in the ground they managed to narrow them down into a tight corner near the edge of the hill, but it was too late as they had drunk poison before they could be taken prisoner and know how to heal Scotch and Mary. Words around the bodies were unfolding to reveal a hidden message.

Only one can escape.

Minx, Kinky, Jeff and Darth made their way back to Scotch and Mary bleeding to their deaths, with the white rice snow around them turning red from their oozing bodies, they moved the bodies away from the cold before they could die from frost bite and any other lurking creatures in the shadows back into the ice castle so Minx could treat their wounds. It wasn't looking good for Scotch as injury after injury it was getting worse for him although he somehow was managing to survive, whereas for Mary nothing appeared to be working from the medicines Minx had in her medical kit as her body temperature was dropping below 5 degrees, they tried keeping her warm with the other spare blankets they found in the guest room.

With the group now running out of resources for themselves Darth and Minx volunteered to keep an eye on Mary and Scotch until they could fully recover, Kinky and Jeff went off to find spare resources in the castle shutting the door behind them covering it in furniture nearby, making sure the close was clear from Coffee if he were still alive or any of his minions could not find and take them hostage. As they walked down the corridor they came across two empty bags which could come in handy to store their findings in making it easier than having to carry food and other resources in their bare hands.

Walking even further down the corridor searching through the different rooms, cupboards, tables and draws they found plenty of clean water, food, medical equipment, and clothes which could last them for 3 months. Footsteps could be heard coming from the other direction causing them to quickly run into the lonely wardrobe standing in the middle of the corridor, waiting patiently for Coffee's minions to go past, once they did and the close was clear they stepped out of the wardrobe and carried on looking for resources, they felt a cold breeze and a faded shadow brush pass them pushing them to the side at a strong force with laughter following it behind.

Kinky and Jeff decided to ignore this and carried on walking around for a little while longer, to see if they could find anymore supplies hanging around before they needed to make their way back to their hide out to help Scotch and Mary still recovering. The strange shadow they spotted next to Jeff was changing shapes and moving as if it had a mine of its own, they ran for their lives splitting up to make the mysterious figure confused as they made their way back to the hidden hide out, shutting the door behind them as the shadow used its force to break in but they moved the closets furniture available to them to block the door from the inside.

Taking a few moments to capture their breath moving the heavy objects from one place to another to slowly make their way down the stairs, when suddenly the stairs, door, and furniture in front of it started to shake making the furniture mountain of tables and chairs fall down rolling down the spiral staircase, knocking Jeff and Kinky coldcocked lying on the stairs. The faceless shadow of the night removed the broken furniture mountain of rubble chairs and tables lifting Jeff and Kinky up in the air by the neck taking off his mask to reveal it was Riley.

The faceless shadow of the night Riley now had Jeff and Kinky in his bare hands throwing them down the stairs with a strong force, Minx and Darth looked on from the other side of the room where they were taking care of Scotch and Mary, both of them stood up and grabbed the nearest objects to them; a machete and sword to the side entrance of the staircase waiting for Riley to enter the room for the trap they had placed. Riley could see through their trap and made his hands go through the walls, gripping onto Darth and Minx throwing them up in the air followed by a punch strong enough it made them bounce across the room. Riley made his way sweeping across the floor towards the weakened Minx taking out his bullets to load the gun in his other hand, pointing it at Minx.

"Any last words?" said Riley.

Minx did not reply as she was knocked out from earlier, Riley laughed moved his hand onto the trigger and shot 5 rounds, Scotch from the other side limped as fast as he could before the bullets could hit Minx and took them all into his chest and with that he had disappeared or that is what they had thought. Jeff and Kinky awoke from their knocked-out moment, rushing to help Minx, Darth, and Scotch, but it was too late for Scotch as all the blood from his body had oozed out making him look like a flatten balloon. It was a huge shock for them all and they had to be prepared for the next time the shadow of the night Riley would strike next and move their location before another raid could take place. They buried Scotch in the kinky room, grabbed their belongings and packed their bags to make their way to the top of the ice castle the roof, as they walked carefully up the stairs taking out the minions and servants on guard working for Coffee. As they got higher on the stairs it would start shaking and they could see why, the stairs were falling apart, they ran as quickly as they could, pushing the enemy trying to kill and prevent them from stopping them in their tracks.

The group had just made it out from the ginormous staircase which was falling apart but at the top of the stairs was no other than Coffee and Riley.

"Kill them!!!" Coffee exclaimed.

Riley and the other shadow of the night men went forth and captured Darth, Minx, Kinky and Jeff after they took out the minions around them and a few shadows but Mary who was still recovering and standing on her two feet stood on her own, taking down as many shadows as she could but the last one Mary encountered was Riley who grabbing her by the neck breaking it and splitting her in two as the others watched from afar. Once she was not moving or showing life Riley dropped the body and made everyone else disappear, while the gang remained with Marys body torn apart.

Chapter 5: A friend lost is a friend gained

With Mary and Scotch both dead and buried beneath their feet, they shall always remain alive in the memories of Kinky, Jeff, Darth, and Minx, they needed a plan to dispose of Riley the shadow knight and servants of Coffee. Although they knew their lives could be at state meaning they too could end up dead, the group needed to make the numbers game of them vs Coffee and his army in the favour of them winning so they could leave the wretched ice castle.

From his high school DXD bag Jeff pulled out a map showing different layers and levels of the castle.

"Kinky and Minx you take the bottom two layers" said Jeff, they nodded in agreement and did so.

"Darth and I will take the last two, once we have all secured and taking control of those areas we will meet at the centre to take out Riley and if enough time overrule Coffee as well" said Jeff while they were running.

With that the two groups split up and heading to their designated areas, pushing the Coffee army territory back, decreasing it by a quarter than what the original number was of 10 million, killing and wounding many of the minions by stealing their mass of destruction weapons and using it for themselves of: mini mortars, machine guns and bombs. All levels were now clear, encountering some hostages of servants and soldiers who refused to help Coffee otherwise known as rebels who have been locked up since the ice castle was first opened to the public in the 60's.

They pledged their alliance and lives to help the group and stop Coffee once and for all, running up the other staircases to all meet up at the centre of the ice castle where Coffee and his minions were. Once they finally arrived at the centre they could see Coffee's army in the distance hurdling together in long rows and many minions splitting themselves into two, at this moment they knew this was going to end horribly as they were outnumbered, it was over.

But they were not going to let it end here, after everything they have been put through, all those who have been killed for them to be alive. Coffee's army rose a red and black pirate flag into the air waving it side to side shouting 'charge', rushing towards the rebels, Kinky, Jeff, Darth, and Minx. They too rushed into battle once they had crossed the middle of the centre; bullets, bombs, arrows, ammunition, ash, blood, crushed bones, and bodies were flying all over the place uncontrollably as if they were dolls being controlled by strings.

They came from the front, they came from the back, they came from the sides and even the air, as both sides were decreasing in numbers they gradually had a clear view of Riley the shadow knight and could execute him, although he was surrounded by other minions he was using as meat shields. They stratagem through the minions and army surrounding Riley finding a blind spot he had left opened and firing three silver rounds through his body.

"One down now we just need to end Coffee" deemed Jeff as his plan had worked.

They could see Coffee just to the far right of them slaughtering the rebels and those who denied joining his army and evil plans.

Cantering as quickly as they could towards Coffee to strike him down to end all of this once and for all. But he had moved out of the way, releasing a weird bright purple beam into the ground killing many people and minions, falling to their knees vulnerable to anything Coffee strike down Jeff and Kinky and with that he and the last remaining minions he had from the fight fled into the darkness.

Jeff with the little life left in him crawled his way to Kinky, with a blood trail scrapping across the floor. Minx and Darth getting back to their feet from the incident moments ago made their way to help Jeff and Kinky, carrying them to the side so Minx could stich up their cuts and wrap them in bandages. With the help of Darth assistance, they managed to get the patients; Kinky, Jeff and other rebels back in one piece, although they were down in numbers Coffee and his minions could strike them again to finish the job, they would have to move on in the castle leaving behind the piles of unknown men and women names and bodies to rot as they would go forth carrying on the fight which was abandoned to the doorstep of Coffee's hideout.

From Jeff's map there was only two places left which could possibly lead them to Coffee's hangout, the attic of the ice castle which would be where Coffee is most likely to be or the actual roof, it would be a suicidal mission, but it was the only way left they were willing to go through. Jeff and Kinky marched to the roof with half of the rebels while Minx and Darth went to the attic with the remaining rebels left behind, they charged down doors and staircases taking full control, pushing back the coffee minions, and taking prisoners to be executed by them later.

The odds were in favour of them to win as the wind which wobbled through the air from the half-broken windows, flew softly against the bodies who laid flatten on the ground or stood with a fighting spirit of a lion. Once the rooms and other places were clear they split off into the two different areas to search for Coffee and end his endless game of bloodshed, both parties at their doors able to hear movement, change of weapons and talking. The only problem they had was who had Coffee behind their door.

Both parties swallowing their nerves down their throats, wiping off the sweat from their heads, preparing to barge into their chosen rooms.

'3, 2, 1'!!!!

BANG!!!

Both sides from the attic and roof fired and charged, noises could be heard below and above, the firing and shots from the attic had stopped, however the shots from the roof would get louder like the beat of a heart thumping, falling silent for a few seconds. Minx and Darth ran up the stairs leading up to the roof of the ice castle, pools of blood dropping all the way down the stairs, splattered on the walls and the room they had entered, Coffee and his minions were there, placing two heads onto spikes before they disappeared once again, the heads belonging to Jeff and Kinky.

What they did not see was the addition of two more heads hanging on the back of the door, Darth's and Minx's with the eyes gouged out and blood pouring out from the different areas circumcised. Talking to herself 'this is just a dream, this is just a dream' Minx awoke drenched in sweat, Kinky, Jeff, Darth and the remaining rebels were all asleep around her at the heart of the warm campfire they had ignited for warmth. She calmed herself down and shortly laid her head back down on her black leather jacket, looking up at the ceiling thinking of life before coming to the ice castle until she finally fell asleep.

As the twinkling stars and moon disappeared behind the sun it was now morning, they all awoke and were ready to strike Coffee, from Jeff's map there was only two places left which could possibly lead them to Coffee's hangout, the attic of the ice castle where Coffee is most likely to be or the actual roof, it would be a suicidal mission, but it was the only way left they were willing to go through. Jeff, Minx, Kinky and Darth marched with half of the rebels left to the other floors left to conquer, charging down doors and staircases taking full control, pushing back the coffee minions, and taking prisoners to be executed by them later, the events which were now taking place were exactly similar to Minx's dream.

"Before we split up, I think we should do men go to the roof while women go to the attic" said Minx calmly trying to stop the same events from her dream to happen.

Without questioning Minx's idea, they did as she asked. Once the rooms and other places were clear they split off into the two different areas to search for Coffee and end his endless game of bloodshed, both parties at their doors able to hear movement, change of weapons and talking. The only problem they had was who had Coffee behind their door, Kinky and Jeff switched places before they proceeded to go in as Minx still anxious did not want one of them to die.

Both parties swallowing their nerves down their throats, wiping off the sweat from their heads and preparing to barge into their rooms. '

3, 2, 1'!!!!

BANG!!!

Both sides from the attic and roof fired and charged, noises could be heard below and above, the firing and shots from the roof had stopped, however the shots from the attic would get louder like beat of a heart thumping, falling silent for a few seconds. Kinky and Darth ran down the stairs leading to the attic of the ice castle, pools of blood dropping all the way down the stairs, splattered on the walls and the room they had entered, Coffee and his minions were there, placing heads onto a spike before they disappeared once again, the heads belonged to Jeff and the fallen rebels.

Minx was left in the room on her own with a few starches and covered in blood, although she had survived and let Kinky live; she unfortunately could not save Jeff.

"And what on earth have you people done to my room!!! Exclaimed Alisha, Darth's ex-girlfriend had finally arrived with her bags.

Darth, Kinky and Minx turned their heads towards the door and could see Alisha, Darth was not impressed as he no longer loved Alisha but Minx, although he was embarrassed to tell her, his face turned bright pink as he started to blush. He quickly ended the silence to hide his blushed face

'Why have you come, two years have passed?' asked Darth

"It just came in the post two weeks ago by a Mr Coffee, which said he was sending it on your behalf, so I got the next flight available to come here."

At that moment they all knew that Alisha had been sent as a trap to distract and find them.

"Did he say anything else?" Asked Darth with a puzzled face.

"Only to keep the letter and use the pen which came included which only works if you press on the top three times." Said Alisha, pulling out the pen and letter from her bag.

"Can I look at that pen for a second?" Asked Darth.

Alisha handed over the pen and it was Darth's worse imaginable thought to happen, the pen had a tracking device which can be triggered if it is pressed three times. Darth threw the pen to the side, stepping on top of it repeatedly until it broke in two, Darth and Minx grabbed Alisha by the arms as Kinky grabbed her bags' running as quickly as they could away from the attic as they could hear small footsteps from the corner and above about to close in on the room. They just managed to escape with their limbs still attached, running room from room, so the hunter minions could not track them by their smell.

The four of them waited until they had gone pass, Alisha had sneezed like a cat chasing after a mouse almost giving away their hiding place in the room opposite the men's bathroom. Darth was starting to blush again as they were in the lady's bathroom, and he was surrounded by three women mainly Minx it was as if he had his own harem in a manga come to life. Once it was clear and the hunter minions had moved further away they made their way, snapping Darth out of his daydreaming fantasy, even though those hunter minions had gone down the hall from the other side as the four of them were popping around the corner of the ice castle corridor, they ran into Coffee with chains in both hands and a necklace filled with the prize possession of his defeated enemy one of them was of Jeff's eyes.

Kinky hastily threw one of Alisha's bags at Coffee and his hunter minions, knocking them over to give herself Darth, Minx and Alisha a bit of time to get away.

"After them you fools'"!!! Exclaimed Coffee.

The hunters dragged out their daggers and ran after them.

"That was my bag" said Alisha, looking upset as it contained her expensive shoes and clothing.

"I'll buy you another pair of shoes once we get out of here and a few more stuff, but you will have to forgive me for what I'm about to do" said Darth.

Darth and Minx threw even more bags and items from her bags, preventing the hunters from chasing after them. Alisha face had turned red with white puffs of cloudy steam could be seen coming out of her ears, as her belonging were being treated as rubbish to be thrown around the place, enraging with anger about to explode like a firework.

The hunters were finally lost, nor could they even track them down due to the shoes and clothing Alisha carried in her luggage being new, they made their way around the other floor to find another way round the hunters without sensing them with Coffee's magic, is what they had thought until a red circle portal emerged from the sides and underneath them, it was Coffee and his minions. They managed to trace them down by a piece of Kinky's hair, one of Coffee's marksman pulled out a trap capture glass from his pocket throwing it in the direction of Kinky spiralling in the air gradually approaching her, Alisha pushed Kinky to the side, absorbed by the trap capture glass, vanishing with Coffee and his troops.

After a few minutes, Kinky arose from the ground after being saved by Alisha from being devoured by the trap capture glass possibly never to be seen again, however falling through the air and attached to a torn piece of clothing belonging to Alisha was a note explaining how; Minx, Darth and Kinky have six hours to find Alisha before the sand trapped in the capture glass tramples her to death. They each read the note and scattered room to room in search for Alisha, they looked far, they looked close by and searched below, but no one could find her. As seconds turned to minutes and minutes into hours, they only had one hour left, where could Alisha be they thought to themselves, as they did not have that much time now remaining. In the distance they could hear a faint sound of someone pleading for help and banging on glass.

Could it be Alisha?

Or possibly a trap set by Coffee, there was only one way to find out and they did not have a choice but to investigate, they followed the sound of the faint banging leading them through different paths, until they came to a halt as the sound of the banging became louder, the only problem was the sound was coming from the ground floor which the staircase to go there had been eradicated from the war. Hunters could be seen scanning the area like a hawk hunting its prey with hybrid wild dogs, prepared to stop Kinky, Darth and Minx from saving Alisha.

How were they going to break in?

How would they get down to the ground floor?

The three of them needed to decide as 25 minutes were remaining.

With the clock ticking, time was at a disadvantage for them, the gang needed to act now before it was too late. As the time in the background ticked furiously down, they needed to make a move otherwise they would be torn into shreds by the hybrid wild dogs lurking below for intruders. Kinky saw an advantage a thin strip line hanging on the opposite side of the rubble where they were hiding with 2 metal hangers to glide across, which will take all of them down to the ground. The only problem was there was 3 of them but 2 metal hangers and they would need to move as quickly and silently as possible without making the hybrid wild dogs and guards knowing they were around.

Darth and Minx went first sharing the metal hanger and holding onto each other tightly so neither of them would fall flat to the ground, Kinky followed. The line holding them was about to break, they needed to jump off the line as soon as they could and with 15 minutes now remaining on the clock before Alisha is killed. They had no other choice if they wanted to save Alisha in time they would have to jump and hope that they land on something soft when they hit the ground. They fell through the air, landing on the ground and avoided breaking any bones or limbs but managed to start a fire which released puffs of smoke into the air alerting the guards on duty.

Once the guards saw the puffs of smoke, they let the hybrid wild dogs free from their leashes to attack the intruders. The gang leaped for their lives splitting up in different directions like headless chicken trying to make the dogs exhausted with the remaining 10 minutes on the clock, this made the hybrid wild dogs more aggressive and chase after them. They could see the hybrid wild dogs were not going to stop and decided to run in the direction to where Alisha was with 5 minutes now remaining, the 3 of them ran as quickly as they could to free Alisha from the Coffee guards on duty.

The plan of running around was starting to pay off as the hybrid wild dogs were starting to get tired, they were now so close to the area Alisha was in, just a few more seconds and they would have saved her in time. More guards with weapons and fresh hybrid wild dogs could be seen from behind as they approached the camp containing Alisha in the trap capture glass. Once the 3 of them reached the camp and got inside, the camp was stocked with different trap capture glasses and reflections of Alisha 2 minute remained on the clock counting down very slowly. They searched thoroughly through the piles of capture glasses, but it was no use each glass they came across would be a decoy or filled with sand.

The clock on the camp wall still counted down, but Darth noticed something odd about the clock, it had been reset as the time was 12:00pm.

They had failed, to save Alisha.

A strange laugh could be heard from behind the piles of capture glasses where Kinky stood, it was Alisha; her behaviour was not the same, her eyes poisoned with anger making them red. Alisha pulled Kinky towards her pulling out a syringe filled with poison striking it at her chest. Darth and Minx tried running towards her, but the guards stopped them. Kinky had died, Alisha's face was happy with joy as she murdered Kinky.

"I did what you asked for" said Alisha.

She was part of Coffees plan from the beginning. Coffee appeared from behind taking the poison syringe away and slicing her in two.

Both Alisha and Kinky were now dead, with both bodies being taking out of the large white camp and thrown into a deep black hole ditch filled with other loss bodies perished from the war they had months ago. Coffee's hunters took Minx and Darth locking them up in steel crystal chains to be thrown into their very own prisons to be tortured. They were tortured; left, right and centre on their scared bodies, with cuts and bruises scattered across their bodies a sight which was not pleasant to look at, not even the human eye. For thirty days, thirty evenings and thirty nights they were prisoners of Coffee being treated like animals to be killed slowly in an attempt to break their spirits, until one night a new prisoner had been brought into Darth's cell by the head prison guard Beazy, the prisoners face covered in a metal mask but the tip of his beard could just be seen, it was Mattk.

Chapter 6: An old friend fight

Beazy removed the metal mask pouring buckets of water on top of Mattk, Mattk was a man with a beard of iron and sharp on the corner giving him the nickname cactus; he was the right hand of Coffee before betraying him in an attempt to murder his close friend, after witnessing Coffee's guards and servants mistreating those who came to the castle just to be kept in cages for Coffee's own entertainment and fun. Once Beazy left the prison cell, Mattk was gasping for air after having buckets of water thrown onto him.

Minx kept her distance as Darth approached Mattk slowly kneeling on one knee to talk to him

"You probably don't like us, nor want to work with us, but with your help we can escape".

Mattk knew all the blueprints and plans of the castle from; hidden doors, traps, where security would be tight and exits to escape the prison.

"It will come with a heavy price or something of equal value in return for helping you two escape from this cell." Replied Mattk.

"Deal you help us escape and we will offer you something in return" said Minx

"Once the head guard comes back at the strike of dawn take his keys and tie him up, from there we will escape through the hidden walls and passages then you two can re pay me" said Mattk.

Dawn was now approaching; the three of them waited in their corners for the head guard Beazy to enter the prison cell and open the door, the lock was turning.

They waited patiently for the person behind the door to enter, preparing to strike them down to obtain the key. The head guard Breezy entered the room with their one piece of bread and bean soup, once he placed the tray down they leaped from their corners and tripped Breezy over, knocking him out with the metal tray and tying him up unable to escape once they break free from their prison cell. They took the keys from his pocket using it to remove their chains and placed them onto Breezy body while he was still out cold. Mattk unlocked their cell door carefully as two guards were waiting on the other side, they needed to get past them without being noticed.

It would be a tough choice either going pass the guards being spotted and killed instantly for attempt of escape or taking them out as well. Minx came up with a better plan, removing Breazy clothes for Mattks to be disguised as the head guard transferring Darth to another cell. The guard fell for the trick as Minx came from behind and stabbed both in the chest to take their clothes, which would allow her and Darth to also blend in without being recognised. They followed Mattk through the hidden tunnels, paths, and doors of Coffee's prison to escape. Darth was amazed by how Mattk had memorised the whole castle prison layout without having to takeout the blueprints from his pocket as they were crawling through the air vents the three of them could hear the guard talking about the execution day 'The end for all heroes' for all prisoners. They decided to stop and hear more about the special day.

"In three days, it will take place and we'll be able to take over the country and world for lord Coffee" the guards burst out laughing.

Darth found the way they laughed extremely funny and decided to join in, a hybrid mouse locus had crawled into Darth's pants causing him to continue laughing uncontrollably, it crawled all around his body and made a few nibble marks in his pants too, the guards below could hear the outbreak of laughter and knew straight away the prisoners had escaped. The guards ran down the hallways setting off the alarms to notify the others, all the secret service Orric guards heard the alarm and prepared to capture or kill all escapees.

Mattk, Minx and Darth crawled as far as they could in the air vents while the guards attempted to roast bake burn them with heat, like a Christmas chicken in the oven. The heat was getting to them, as a stream of sweat could be seen on their clothes, the path ahead was blocked so were all the other options, they would have to stick to escaping through the air vents before it becomes unbearable for them. Crawling even further in the scorching air vent to an exit for three of them to climb down, they walked through the dark shadows avoiding the Orric guards hunting for them. Minx took out her mini pick pocket key, to see if she could open any of the doors, they strolled passed to obtain extra supplies for when they need to camp. A light underneath the storage room crates could be seen poking its head around for them to see, Mattk remembered what the lights below were, their path to escaping the castles prison.

One by one the three of them dropped below and resealed the crack to be unnoticed by others. The underground tunnel was filled with spider webs rotting with decay on the cold brick walls and smelt of urine mixed with other deadly substances, harmful enough to kill them, Darth ripped one of his spare shirts Minx carried in her bag and handed everyone a piece to cover their mouth and nose, as Mattk led them deeper and deeper the beaming lights around to guide them were starting to weaken and more weirder noises could be heard as if they were in an arena.

They scanned through the tiny crack to see what was happening, the noises would roar with excitement and rage as public executions for the final day were beginning, chopping off the heads of many prisoners chosen randomly, blood could be seen piling on top of each other, layer upon layer like red velvet cake as more bodies were executed, they could see the prisoners had nothing in common to why they were chosen for the final day apart from being all locked away to rot in Coffee's prison for years. Mattk could hear Coffee approaching the building from the other side on his horse who he'd refer to as his little pony due to it being the best in the world and the only dragon horse around, they were going to stop the final day by sabotaging the event, before the main event takes place.

Only a few hours before the main event takes places, the crowd getting wilder as people were being killed, three guards separately came by and in one go they knocked them out with sleep darts, placing their bodies in the explosive/ gun power closet pilling on top of each other like a man mountain. They took the explosives/gun powder from the room and disguised themselves in the Orric guard clothes plotting the explosives around the venue in areas no one would care to look. Once it was time and Coffee was about to announce the main event, they were ready to destroy the building and coffee.

3, 2, 1.

They set the match on fire and ignited the powder it spread quickly like a headless chicken, but something was not making the building, arena or crowd stands burn to a crisp, it instead did nothing.

"You must have thought I was a fool" said Coffee, laughing his head off.

"That was not an explosive substance but instead my next weapon and thanks to you it will now come into action, guards seal the doors, entrances and exit!!! Exclaimed Coffee.

Mattk, Minx and Darth looked back puzzled to what Coffee had meant. Coffee teleported Mattk and cut his arms off, dropping droplets of blood onto the weird seeds/powder. The ground started to break and the bodies that were executed earlier jumped up onto their feet.

"We could have ruled the world together Mattk, had everything we always wanted". Said Coffee

"My man-eating zombies are alive"!!!! Shouted coffee, pushing Mattk down the steps of his stage to the pit full of zombies.

The zombies gazed at Mattk from the horizon looking deep at his thumping heart, sticking out their tongues to lick their blood-filled face as they were about to devour him alive. Minx and Darth could only look on as the zombies rushed towards Mattk within seconds gobbling him up into their endless pit stomachs.

"Don't look so surprised, you're both next" said Coffee sipping his hot cup of cappuccino.

Coffee's Orric guards pushed both of them into the pit, landing on their bottoms. Among the zombies about to come charging at them they could see some familiar faces, their old companions on this holiday adventure to the ice castle for a holiday not a horrific time. You could tell from the look on Coffee's face that he was very amused that finally his enemies Minx and Darth who were still standing would soon be dead, deleted from existence, thanks to them awakening his zombies. The zombies grew ever so closer to them, just a few more steps and they would be eradicated. Darth and Minx picked up the rocks, stones, rubble, spears anything they could find poking out of the ground for them to use against those vile beasts, it was effective, but they grew angrier than the last and came charging from different sides.

"Enough"!!! Said Coffee he pulled back the zombies making a wall separating them from the zombies.

"Since the both of you like fighting, you both will compete for your lives, the winner takes all and shall leave the castle. While the loser is trapped here forever by submission, quitting or DEATH" said Coffee

The battle of no return was about to begin.

Chapter 7: The battle of no return

The battle of no return games, the final stage of survival was about to begin, Darth and Minx looked at each other through the see-through walls dividing them. You could see in their eyes they did not want to fight each other as they cared for each other dearly, more than anything in the world. No other options were available, protesting would just mean they would be killed instantly. Coffee arose from his seat and made the wall disappear, the games were on their way. Both Minx and Darth picked their fighting weapons, and the duel began, Minx took the first shot hitting Darth on the chest, almost cutting him open.

Darth could see he would need to do more, if he wanted to win the fight against Minx but keep her alive. Jab, spear, slice, flying chicken bones in the air, these two put their love for each other aside and fought like they have never fought before. Coffee could see he was not going to get a clear winner, stroking his beard he released some zombies which looked like their friends. He thought making their companions come back as zombies would put them off, it was effective. Minx and Darth did not want to fight the zombies but would need to if they had to survive. Growing much angrier with frustration his beard turning gingery gold like a biscuit Coffee decided to manipulate and play mind tricks on both to find a winner.

"Minx you know he is weak, use your strategies and his weakness of his love for you to kill him" said Coffee

"Darth she is weak and vulnerable, finish her, she does not love you, she never did, she just used you" said Coffee.

Both Minx and Darth fought with pure hatred for each other, their love for another, fading away into the darkness. Darth decided enough was enough and went charging like a bull at Minx with daggers in his hands, Minx was just cut by his daggers across her shoulders, before Darth could turn his whole body around. Minx stabbed him through his open chest with the spear, whispering in his ear before he fell to the ground that she was sorry.

Coffee could see Minx had won the fight, meaning Darth must die.

"It surprises me that after all that time you let her win by your mind being corrupted with hate Darth and you cared for her, considering she was my secret weapon from the beginning" said Coffee

"Don't listen to him, he's lying" said Minx.

As she rushed to Darth's body to comfort him. But Coffee was telling the truth, Minx was his weapon to find out their locations and areas they hid. Coffee picked up a dagger from the ground and threw it in the direction of Minx, striking her in the back.

"Just one more thing, the daggers and weapons are covered in poison and there's only one anecdote to use." Said Coffee throwing it on the ground.

As the anecdote was twisting and twirling in the air, Darth and Minx with their final breath leaped towards the anecdote to stop it from reaching the ground and grabbing it in their hands. Darth stretched his hand out even further just catching the anecdote before it could reach the ground, he jumped over to Minx offering her the anecdote, but she refused to take it and suggested Darth should have it instead. This went on for quite a while until neither of them could decide who should take the anecdote and be the one to live on.

The anecdote bottle did not contain a lot as most of the liquid was leaking from the bottom of the glass container, only one of them could consume the liquid and they were running out of time as only 1/5 of the bottle remained. They decided to split the remaining amount into equal amounts for the two of them to stop the poison from spreading. Only to find out that what they had consumed was a potion to turn them against each other.

"Kill them now!!!" shouted Coffee from the top of his lungs.

Coffee's guards could be seen rushing towards them, they had nowhere to escape and no more energy in them to fight, all they could do was remain where they were and hope they would have a splendid send off. The guards approached even closer with their daggers getting even lower ready to strike them down for the last time.

A white flash appeared along with an old man with a white curly beard pulling both of them off the ground and into the flash.

"Hurry after them, before it's too late"

The guards tried their hardest to catch up to them but failed just by a few inches as they could not reach Minx, Darth, and the mysterious figure in time to capture them.

"Find and bring them back to the castle, I want them bought back alive" shouted Coffee.

The guards gathered all their equipment and went searching for the escapees. The reward bounty for their capture had been increased to 600,000 pieces of gold and 400,000 pieces of chicken, to tempt all the villagers and hunters nearby to get involved in the search and look for them.

Meanwhile hundreds of miles away in a cave, Minx and Darth were still recovering from the incident in the castle, they had been asleep for 13 days and getting better very slowly being looked after by the mysterious figure who saved them. They finally woke up with the poison almost out of their system, but they no longer knew who the other person lying in the bed was, apart from being saved by a mysterious figure from Coffee.

The mysterious figure had prepared a meal for the two of them, a meal big enough to feed a whole castle on the small table, a green verse could be seen on the table which looked like a bottle of 7UP but was actually a potion to help them with their recovery and restore them to full health. Minx and Darth both gazed out the window nearby to see where they were, all they could see was a lot of green fresh fields and tiny villages in the distance, they were inside a cave on top of the mountain. They were quite surprised by how far up they were and how they could almost see everything, it was almost like they had crossed over to the other side again.

"You should have something to eat, before it disappears" said the mysterious figure stuffing his face down with food.

They both took a seat at the small table and began to eat the food prepared by the figure.

"Who are you and why did you save us?" Asked Darth, stuffing pieces of fried chicken dipped in gravy down his mouth.

The mysterious figure looked up to him.

"I thought you would have realised by now who I am" said the mysterious figure

The mysterious figure started to remove the clothing from his face, layer by layer revealing who he finally was.

It was Jasper.

Darth Riskins older cousin Jasper had saved them from Coffee, the same person who had tried to slaughter them while they were in the castle and was working with Coffee….

Printed in Great Britain
by Amazon